W9-AXG-910

Title: Snowy Matsushima
Year: 2007
Dye plants: acorn, indigo
Collection: Private collection

Title: Evening Faces
Year: 2003
Dye plants: *shikon (lithospermum purpurocaerula)*, harlequin glorybower
Collection: The Museum of Modern Art, Shiga

Title: *Suma*
Year: 2002
Dye plants: rose, *soyogo* (*ilex pedunculosa*), cape jasmine
Collection: The Museum of Modern Art, Shiga

Title: *Biwakou*
Year: 2000
Dye plants: bayberry, onion
Colleciton: Private collection

Title: Wind in the pines
Year: 2003
Dye plants: indigo, *kariyasu* (*miscanthus tinctorius*)
Collection: The Museum of Modern Art, Shiga

Title: Autumn Excursion
Year: 2000
Dye plants: sappanwood, bayberry, *kariyasu* (*miscanthus tinctorius*), indigo
Collection: Private collection

Title: Evening Mist
Year: 2001
Dye plants: black dye, acorn
Collection: Private collection

Title: Morning Glory
Year: 2001
Dye plants: indigo, *kariyasu* (*miscanthus tinctorius*)
Collection: The Museum of Modern Art, Shiga

The Music of Color
Shimura Fukumi

photography by Inoue Takao

translated by Matt Treyvaud

The Music of Color
Shimura Fukumi. Photographs by Inoue Takao.
Translated by Matt Treyvaud

Published by
Japan Publishing Industry Foundation for Culture (JPIC)
3-12-3 Kanda-Jinbocho, Chiyoda-ku, Tokyo 101-0051, Japan
First English edition: March 2019

© 1998 by Fukumi Shimura and Takao Inoue
English translation © 2017 by Japan Publishing Industry Foundation for Culture
Introduction to the English Edition © Takashina Shuji

All rights reserved
Originally published in the Japanese language under the title of *Iro wo kanaderu* on December 3, 1998 by Chikumashobo Ltd.

English publishing rights arranged directly with Shimura Fukumi and Inoue Takao

Book design by Kasai Kaoru and Nakamoto Yoko
Typesetting: Andrew Pothecary (itsumo music)
Production: Ueda Aki (Pont Cerise)

Printed in Japan
ISBN 978-4-86658-061-6
http://www.jpic.or.jp/japanlibrary/

Preface to the English Edition   Takashina Shūji

Shimura Fukumi is widely known as a master of plant-based dyes and *tsumugi-ori* weaving, with her achievements in the latter field earning her the official title "Preserver of Important Intangible Cultural Properties"—or, more colloquially, "Living National Treasure." The artworks she creates are like jewels, intricately combining the colors of natural flora with the patterns of *tsumugi-ori*.

Plant-based dyes are drawn from flower, fruit, and branch, but dyeing with them is not as simple as is generally supposed. For example, simmering sakura (cherry blossom) petals in full bloom does not produce the delicate color of the flowers themselves. But when Shimura tried simmering a branch received when "powdery snow was still falling" from an old man pruning sakura in the foothills of Mount Ogura, an experience she describes in this book, the result was "a dye that turned the fabric such a beautiful pink it seemed to fill my room with the fragrance of the blossoms." In a bough that seemed to die as it was cut from the trunk, there yet lived what can only be the spirit of the sakura. After more than twenty years of experimentation, Shimura has come to feel that the very life of plants is expressed through color.

Color is also used to convey meaning in our own everyday lives— think of the red, yellow, and green of traffic lights. In that respect, colors are like words. Words are used to convey meaning too, but in the hands of a superior poet they become lines and verses that speak directly to human sensibility and feeling. In the tenth-century *Kokin wakashū*, the first imperial anthology of Japanese poetry, compiler Ki no Tsurayuki declared, "Japanese poetry has the human heart as its seed and grows into myriad leaves of words." In other words, Japanese poetry consists in words born of "the human heart"—the various thoughts and feelings of people. Essential for this process is the technique (*waza*) of the poet, which shapes the echoes and rhythms of language according to the rules to create works of art.

This *waza* was the basis on which poets competed in the *uta-awase* (poetry contests) of the Heian and Kamakura periods, roughly the ninth through fourteenth centuries.

In the case of Shimura Fukumi, it is her *waza* in the fields of dyeing and weaving that allow her to create art with dyes representing the life force of the plants they are drawn from. Technique like this cannot be faked: it must be attained through dedicated practice. Or, as Shimura herself puts it, "one wrong thread in a hundred, in a thousand, stops the weaving in its tracks."

This superlative skill, for which Shimura was recognized as a Living National Treasure, combines with her honed sensitivity to the appeal of those colors bearing the vitality of nature to permit the stunning world of Shimura's art to emerge. This book is a collection of essays penned over the years by Shimura, a poet and creator of color and textile, but so rich are its observations, so elegant its tone that it might be more accurately described as a book of deeply moving poetry.

Contents

The Music of Color

The Lives of Plants

"Plants are living beings created by nature, just as we are. The grasses and trees we make dyes from offer their lives for our sake, becoming colors that protect us from evil spirits. We must approach them with compassion, and our devotion to the work of dyeing must begin with gratitude and prayers to the *kodama*—the 'spirits of the trees.'"

These are the words of the "Tradition of the Dyers," passed down orally since ancient times and recorded in Maeda Ujō's book *Ancient Colors and Dyes of Japan* (*Nihon kodai no shikisai to some*). Our ancestors, Maeda explains, used medicinal plants with powerful *kodama* to dye clothing for protection from evil. Fires for simmering were lit with reverence; water, earth, and metal were chosen with care; and so the best dyes combined all five of the traditional Asian elements of wood, fire, earth, metal and water. The life in every color came from the root of heaven and earth.

But this tradition of prayerful dyeing was not to last. Today, we feel self-conscious even speaking of *kodama*.

There is no end to the harm humans do to nature, and yet nature still gives more to us than we could ever understand, bending silently to our will. The *kodama* seem insubstantial and fading to us today, and yet those spirits of the plants are ready as ever to offer up their living colors at our command.

The five elements are polluted now, withered at the root. Is it still within our power to keep the ancient dyers' traditions alive?

In the years since I entered the dyer's way, I have received color without limit from the natural world—a flood too great for this meager vessel to contain. Like a joyful child with a new set of paints, I have spent my days dyeing and weaving with the gifts of the grasses and trees.

The idea of praying to the *kodama* never entered my mind, but I did begin to wonder where the endless array of hues came from— whether these colors were not just colors; whether another world entirely might lie behind them.

And then, one day, I had a mystical experience. I tumbled right into that other world.

Like peering through a door that was just ajar, I caught a glimpse of early autumn sunlight and a deep forest that shimmered in the breeze. The leaves were beginning to turn, each one dyed with the utmost care, and the woods were filled with unearthly light. I did not see the spirits of the plants, but I sensed them all around me, and felt the exultation of union with their presence.

I never saw that forest again, but I remember it vividly to this day. To this day I believe that if we can still our hearts enough for the lives of the grasses and trees to reach us, we will realize of our own accord how precious they are.

"Field of Deep Grass" (Fukakusano)

Waste silk

Receiving color

Receiving Color

Sometimes people tell me about attempts at dyeing gone awry. I wanted *this* color, they say, so I used *that* plant, just like the book said, but the result wasn't what I expected.

This has it backwards, I think. The colors we receive are already there, within the plants. Our task is simply to bring them across to our side unharmed, and give them somewhere to stay.

In winter, trees stand in the snow, stoically waiting for spring and preparing to send forth new shoots when it arrives. When we take their trunks and branches for dyeing, we accept without reservation the colors we find within and bring them to life in our weaving. Anything less would be a sin against nature. Every branch on a Japanese plum tree (*ume*) is densely covered in buds that were to be the blossoms of early spring, and this is the life that we receive. It is the color of a thousand, ten thousand plum branches—their statement to the world.

It falls to us to heed that statement and bring that very color to life. We cannot blend it with others—cannot combine the plum and the sakura to create a new color. That would be a crime against the trees, because their colors are more than just colors.

With artificial dyes, things are just the opposite. New colors can be created by mixing. An unmixed color has nothing to ground it. Artificial colors can be bleached, but plant-based dyes cannot. This is the difference between human and natural agency.

The Scent of Sakura

Powdery snow was still falling when I visited the foothills of Mount Ogura one year. There I met an old man who gave me one of the branches he was pruning from the sakura trees. Back in my studio, I simmered it into a dye that turned the fabric such a beautiful pink it seemed to fill my room with the fragrance of the blossoms. At that moment, I experienced what it was like to smell a color. Not as an actual scent, of course, but because all of our senses seem to be connected at some deep level, elements of beauty perceived through one sense resonate subtly across the rest as well.

That day left me longing to dye with sakura again. However, as you might expect from the Japanese saying, "Only a fool cuts a sakura tree, but only a fool *doesn't* cut a plum tree," I never had the opportunity to cut another bough myself. When I received word that plans were afoot to trim the sakura near Ōmi ahead of the September typhoons, I practically flew to the scene to receive some prunings. However, the dye I got from them did not have the same "fragrance" as before. The color was the same gray-tinged pink, but it lacked the previous batch's radiance. Pondering this difference, I realized that plants, too, have their cycles. In late winter, when I had received the branch from Mount Ogura, the sakura had been preparing within its trunk to bloom to the tips of every bough.

That color was the very spirit of the sakura, I thought. It was a deeply moving idea. Close attention later confirmed that the plum and *kariyasu* grass had the same moment, just before they came into bloom or ripen at the head, when their spirit, the color they held within, was at its peak. This should have been obvious, on reflection. When spinning yarn into thread, we use our saliva to wet the strands, and thread spun by a young girl is said to have an entirely different luster from that spun by an old woman. So it goes for all living things.

I once spoke of these matters with Ōoka Makoto, who considered them with his rich poetic sensitivity and wrote them up as an essay called "The Power of Words" (*Kotoba no chikara*). Beautiful speech, correct speech, he writes, is more than just the vocabulary it contains. When someone speaks, their words carry their whole world. Each fleeting utterance reflects the entire person who utters it.

We draw the colors of the sakura not from the petals but from the gnarled bark and branch. Ōoka found this quite surprising, but the blossoms have already bloomed, so no color can come from there. It is the spirit of the tree entire, alive with ceaseless activity, that emerges in the hue of each petal, so different from the trunk—and do we not see the same truth in our struggle to express ourselves with the "petals" that are our words?

If we keep this in our thoughts, then every word, however slight, is an opportunity to experience the vast meaning within that very slightness. That experience, Ōoka concludes, brings us closer at last to speech that is beautiful and correct.

The scent of sakura

Dew from the Trunk

Every year, at the beginning of February, I receive a truck bed full of prunings from the plum groves at Kameoka. They come bundled by age, from fresh green boughs to rugged old branches. All are covered in tiny flower buds, like pearls, some just beginning to blossom. I burn half of the old branches and make lye with the ash, then use that lye to simmer the green boughs for dye.

The initial crimson from the branches, faintly tinged with yellow, slowly reddens within the tree's own lye until a more innocent crimson is born. The branches with their buds still attached gleam within the silk yarn steeping in the dye, almost seeming to blossom there. Although I do this every year, each time it brings me more joy than one person could possibly deserve.

One year, on a late autumn visit to the Shirane Tōgen Museum of Art in Yamanashi, I was struck by the fall colors of the grapevine trellises that covered the slopes. The ground was carpeted in beautiful fallen leaves, and peach orchards stretched into the distance from both sides of the road. How beautiful they must be when they come into bloom, I thought, and wondered aloud what sort of colors they might offer to dye with. The member of the museum staff who was with me must have remembered this, because some time later they sent me a hemp bag full of vineyard and orchard cuttings.

It seems cruel, but dyeing with plants just before they come into bloom, when they are still storing up nutrients within their trunks for that purpose, gives colors of indescribable innocence, like the very spirits of the flora. Those early spring branches were a priceless gift to me, and I immediately set about dyeing with them.

The peach branches were still covered in fluffy buds, and the following morning they dyed the yarn a clear, refined, pale pink. Again, that color could only be called the spirit of the peach itself.

The grapevines I simmered for two days until the liquid was completely wine-colored with a sweet perfume. This, I thought, must be what the ancient purple dye known as *ebizome* was like. The yarn that came out of the pot had a grape-colored hue richer than I had ever seen before. My heart beat faster as I imagined the kimono I could weave with it.

The plum, the peach, the grapevine: without fail, each one births its own color. Whatever assistance we provide in bringing this heavenly dew to earth, the silk yarn drinks these natural essences into the fullness of its being with astonishing stillness. Gazing at the dried rings of yarn placed side by side, I almost heard the trees and vines whispering, in voices only audible this season, and singing quietly in a round. In a different dimension, in an utterly different form, yet somehow entirely unchanged, the lives of the plants descended in gentle chains from the ceiling of my workshop to its every corner, endlessly murmuring soft and low.

Yarn dyed with Bungo plum

Top: Plum flowers
Bottom: Making mordant ash from plum branches

The Timbres of the Wild

After a winter of heavy snows, the greens of a Kyoto spring seem vivid enough to make our eyes water. Our joy in the rebirth of the meadows and fields is all the greater in years like this, as it would be to residents of some northern clime.

Yomogi (Japanese mugwort), *gennoshōko* (dewdrop cranesbill), *rengesō* (Chinese milk vetch), *itadori* (Japanese knotweed), even *karasunoendō* (garden vetch)—this year I dyed with them all. It was the first time I had experimented with the last three, and my view of garden vetch in particular changed entirely. I had always treated it as a nuisance that grew too densely in the garden, but now I found something about its slightly yellowish green impossible to ignore. Even a stroll through the meadows kept my eyes busy now.

As I gazed at the bundles of yarn dyed with these wild plants, they seemed to me the colors of the fields themselves. Light purple tones tinged with browns and grays, a flat scale: that was the cranesbill. Delicately trilling greens and pale yellows: Chinese milk vetch. Resonant grays with stylish blue-green counterpoint: Japanese mugwort. Inspired by the thought of that elegant, muted green in a striped kimono, I ran back to the fields, plucked some more mugwort, and simmered up another batch of dye. Feats like this are only possible in spring, inspiring gratitude for the very idea of seasons.

The color of the earth when it relaxes after the frozen winter and new shoots appear in its embrace; the color of the seedlings, hesitant in the first sunlight they have ever felt; if we could only hear those timbres at the same time, we would realize that the yarn we dye hums with both color and sound—the song of wild flora, newly born.

Broad beans fatten in pods overnight. Spotted bellflowers suspend their white lanterns in the long grass. By dawn, the season has shifted dramatically.

Among these changes, humans, too, enjoy some kind of cellular rebirth, making new spring discoveries. As the milk vetch and cranesbill sprout in the fields, our bodies, our senses keep pace, changing little by little overnight so that we are not left behind as the fields slowly move from spring to early summer.

Returning from my stroll, I take a turn around the garden to see how it is coming along this year. I find the *shimotsuke* (*Spiraea japonica*) covered in tiny blooms and the *yusuraume* (downy cherry) drooping with plump red fruit, as if they had been waiting for me.

Passionflower is something rarer. I was disappointed when the small pot of passionflowers I received withered over the winter—but the soil must have been very good, because they seem to be greening again before my very eyes, tendrils reaching in all directions, dotted with over a hundred budding blossoms. I check them every day until the morning I find a single breathtaking bloom open within the verdant growth. I wonder who gave this plant its Japanese name: *tokeisō*, "clockflower." It does look like something commissioned from a master artisan by a poet after glimpsing the inside of a clock.

The passionflower's delicate but magnificent central structure, ringed by slender papery strands of purple and white, truly seems capable of keeping time, only waiting for some gnome to come along and wind it up.

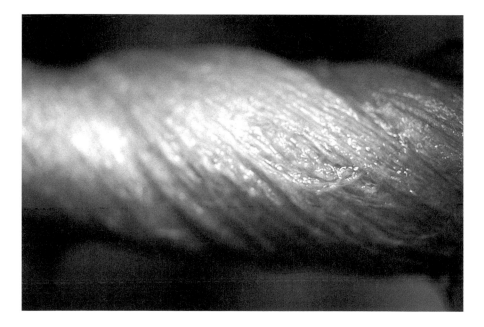

Dyeing with rengesō *(Chinese milk vetch)*

The *Kariyasu* of Mount Ibuki

Every year in late August, just after the Bon festival, I visit Mount Ibuki where the *kariyasu* grass (*Miscanthus tinctorius*) is just starting to send up seed heads.

There is no finer preliminary dye or "bottom" than *kariyasu* for dyeing fabric green. Its blue-tinged gold disappears into the indigo vat only to become a dazzling green when the piece is pulled back out. It is like a birth: not surprising that the Japanese word for "newborn," *midorigo*, literally means "green child." *Kariyasu* lays the foundation for that green, silently playing its part without ever revealing itself directly.

One year, we arrived at Mount Ibuki, harvested all the *kariyasu* we could under the autumn sun, spread it out to dry on the slopes while we ate our lunch and took a nap, and then made our way home with our mountain of kariyasu along with bouquets of *yomogi* (Japanese mugwort), *gennoshōko* (dewdrop cranesbill), *waremoko* (great burnet), *torikabuto* (monkshood), and *kawara nadeshiko* (fringed pink), breathing in the stifling scent of cut grass.

That year's *kariyasu* gave such stunning results that I simply had to praise it in verse, expressing my gratitude for its quiet work behind the scenes creating such beautiful colors.

The Kariyasu *of Ibuki*

On the slopes of Mount Ibuki,
Amid the fields of susuki *grass*
That shine white, red, and gold,
You stood together,
Hesitantly raising meager ears
And swaying in the wind.

The autumn sky that day
Rose far above the mountain's high, high peak,
Cloudless in all directions
As youths in hang-gliders
Soared serene as birds.

The golden fronds of the susuki
Were hung with gilded grains that rang
Like bells across the fields; and
The red susuki *and the* waremokō *in the grass*
Were bright and rich as if freshly lacquered.

The mass of white ears
Was light itself, embodied,
And within it, only you,
In your corner of the field, quietly
Stored up your gold.

When the evening sun began to sink,
All this became
A gorgeous maki-e* *landscape,*
And you were gone, without even
A soul to notice.

But now
Your stalks and leaves and ears have given their all
And been reborn.
This thread, its gold
Run deeply through with blue,
Can only be called sublime.

Eventually you will sink into the dark indigo vat,
And then, as a newborn child of green,
Catch everyone's eye.
But no one will know
That you are there.

O kariyasu of Ibuki!
You shine where no eyes see;
I cannot help but sing your praise.
You are golden drops of autumn sun.

Maki-e: A traditional Japanese craft technique for creating gold or silver designs on a lacquer surface.

On Mount Ibuki

When indigo is combined with kariyasu *(*Miscanthus tinctorius*), green is born*

Gardenia Yellow

December brings the gift of gardenia fruit.

The first thing I do with these beads of golden light is put them on display in my *tokonoma* alcove, piled on a wooden tray. After this, I thread them on long loops of white yarn to hang from the wooden lattice outside my front door. Those that are already ripe, I simmer for dye at once. This has become a yearly ritual for me.

Gardenia is almost too bright, too free of shadow. Unlike other dyes, it requires no mordant—is unaffected by it entirely, in fact, remaining the same shining yellow. Or gold, if you like: a royal color. A king moves for no man. But permitting no other color to approach means solitude, and loneliness.

Every color has its own destiny, and that of *Gardenia jasminoides* echoes its name in Japanese: *kuchinashi*, "no-mouth." It finds its highest beauty in the silence of pure yellow cloth, unmarked by any pattern or design.

Gardenia fruit

The Life of Indigo

Every vat of indigo is a life in full. It begins with the choice of lye,·
often seen as the fluid body or blood of the indigo. From there,
endless conditions combine to direct the life of the vat: the condition
of the *sukumo* (fermented indigo leaves), the thoughts of the dyer, the
weather, the season. From its birth to its final end, a vat of indigo is
very like a human life.

Those early days of shining pale blue, when the indigo is in
high spirits and the "flower" of froth first rises call this childhood
through early youth. Soon, however, the indigo begins to grow calmer,
subsiding with every tide until it seems to have an almost spiritual
inner stability. This is when the color is in its prime; this is when
Japanese indigo shows its deepest and most characteristic hue. But it is
an autumnal beauty, and before long, the vat's final years are upon it.

The "flower" in the indigo grows smaller and less lustrous day by
day, but without giving up its dignified presence at the center of the
vat. At this stage, the color no longer tries to outdo what it achieved
the previous day. Even repeated dyeing does not deliver much in the
way of results. Slowly the indigo retreats, protecting what it has, but it
cannot hide the notes of advancing age that show in it more strongly
by the day.

This marks the first appearance of the quiet, dignified color known
as *kame-nozoki*—"a peek into the vat." By now, the floating "flower"
looks like a small bun on an elderly woman's head. Soon even this
disappears, but the *kame-nozoki* remains. Fabric steeped in the liquid
and then pulled out has a dirty light brown look to it, but this rinses
off to reveal the pale indigo beneath.

I am always quietly moved to see this final color swim into view
within the water. If it were a sound, it would be the faintest of
whispers; if a scent, the perfume of a stranger passing by. And yet,
there it is, undeniably present in the yarn: *kame-nozoki*, the color at
the end of indigo's life.

The newborn indigo

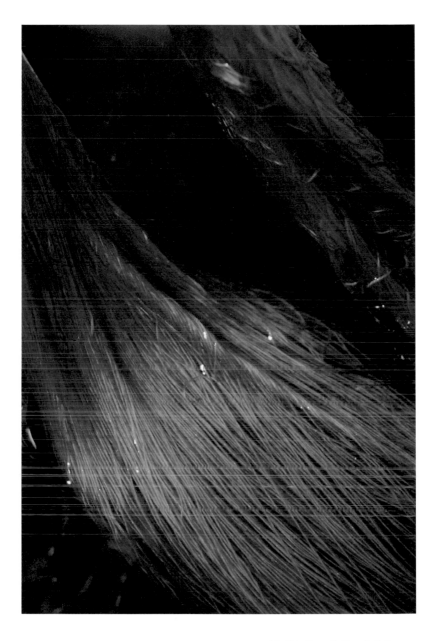

The light blue called hanada *in Japanese*

The Color Green

No plant will give you green dye. Given the abundance of verdant foliage in our world, this might seem mysterious, as if the gods had overlooked some important detail. But I have suspected for some time that it is not an oversight but a puzzle, crafted to convey a deeper truth.

There is no green dye as such, but you can get the color green by combining yellow and blue. Take yarn dyed once with *kuchinashi* (gardenia), *kariyasu* (*Miscanthus tinctorius*), or *kihada* (Amur cork) and dip it into the indigo vat, and green is born. Yes, "born"—this is the expression I always use for green, even as I speak of other colors being "dyed." In Japanese, a newborn is called a *midorigo*—literally "green child"—and somehow this word always comes to mind when I see that green emerge from the vat of indigo.

Perhaps this is because green has such a deep connection to life. It is the forefront of life itself. All living creatures treasure that spark, praying for just one day longer, and yet moment by moment each life marks the time until death. The process never stops. What better color to represent that vital force than green?

You *can* squeeze a green liquid from leaves, but it quickly begins to lose its color until only gray remains. Green is the best symbol of this fleeting life as well. There are pigments and paints that do not have even fleeting life, of course: mineral greens, like verdigris, and the *byakuroku* ("white-green") made from malachite.

Another mystery: If you dye white yarn in an indigo vat, it will be a brownish color when first drawn out. But, as soon as we relax our hands after wringing the yarn dry with bamboo poles, the parts exposed to air begin to turn a vivid emerald green—which soon fades, even as we watch, to be replaced by the light blue called *hanada* in Japanese.

Where does the green that first comes out of the indigo vat go? Does it travel to the "far shore," the afterlife, as the counterpart there of our *hanada*? Are they two sides of the same color, one here and one there? If so, the green that comes from combining blue with yellow is a natural color born at the hands of humanity. Green vanishes, becoming blue; blue vanishes, becoming green. A mystery, as if shuffling dimensions.

Blue is the color of the sky and the sea, as far as our eyes can reach. The ultramarine of the ocean's expanse, the cerulean blue of the above: these are intangible, colors without color. Where do these blues come from that dye the oceans and tint the sky? In Buddhist cosmology, the myriad colors are born when the light from beyond heaven illuminates the three thousand worlds.

Each sunrise, heaven and earth are enveloped in golden light. At nightfall, a blue curtain descends to divide them. The vast cycle of nature teaches us that the color closest to light is yellow, while blue is nearest to darkness. It is yellow and blue that are the two primary colors—the two poles between which the infinite hues reside.

When we use plants to dye with, we are joining in this cycle in some small way. But in even the tiniest of natural phenomena, the deepest teachings of the gods are revealed.

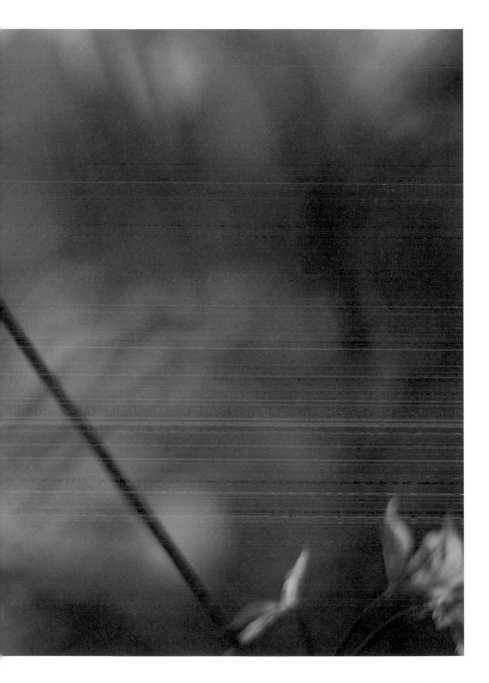

The color green

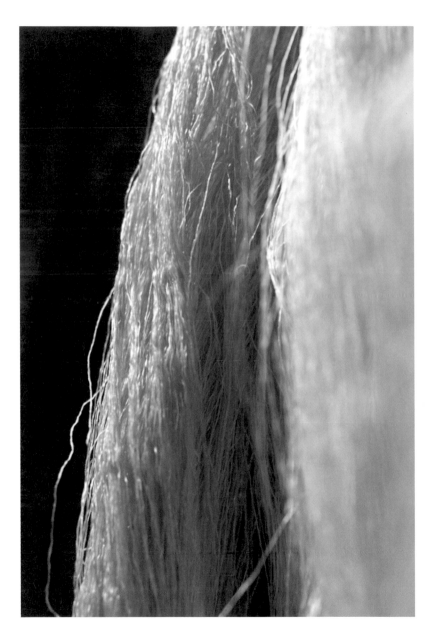

Indigo yarn

Blue and green

The warp and weft

"Ise"

Colors of the sky and sea

On Looms

The warp of a loom is *tate* in Japanese, written using the same character as the word for "sutra" (経). You cannot ignore a flaw in the warp. One wrong thread in a hundred, in a thousand, stops the weaving in its tracks. Try to let it slide—"it's just one thread"—and the wound remains in the fabric forever. As a metaphor for life, this is somewhat frightening.

For someone as clumsy and inclined to half-measures as I am, the way of the loom should have been a very painful trial. For some reason, though, I have walked it all my life. My own faults remain unamended, but I have compensated by letting my heart dance to the mysteries of both sutra and loom, which are more than sufficient.

Another view of the loom sees it as Yin and Yang. The warp is Yin, tradition; the weft is Yang, our everyday lives. Weave them together, and yarn becomes fabric.

The paths of our lives, too, have something like the warp of the loom. Call it destiny, call it fate—in any case, we are helpless to change it. But we are free to weave our weft threads as we like. The full span of our emotions is in the weft, from our darkest moments to our brightest.

If the warp is male, the weft is female. When the warp has powerful, nearly perfect stripes, white weft threads go entirely unnoticed. Only the stripes catch the eye. But it is the steadiness—or sincerity?—of the white weft that allows it to step back and bring the warp to life. It is something like the relationship between the traditional "good husband and virtuous wife," perhaps—or perhaps the weft is another self, loyal to the part of ourselves that we believe in.

White weft

Melodies of Color

Weaving on a loom sometimes feels like strumming a harp. Tones seem to ring out one by one as I bring each color in. The warp is the pattern and the weft the overarching theme that plays against it.

First, I try stripes exactly the same as the warp's. A lattice. Slowly I begin to break the lattice down. Negative space. Thick stripes, thin stripes, no stripes. Irregular, like natural breathing. A uniform look, but without uniformity; the appearance of chaos, but somehow controlled. Spaces that are hard to explain. I weave on, increasingly confident. One step more, one step more . . . Yes—stop there.

The body hears the rhythm spoken by the soul, scoops it up as it flows into space with the lightness of breath, and redirects it into the weaving. With the pulse still quivering like jelly about to set, the next melody is born. Film advancing frame by frame. A natural, unbroken chain.

Unsure whether harmony (color) or rhythm (space) comes first, I pursue and am pursued by both, casting the shuttle as soon as it touches my hand. It feels like improvising a song to a predetermined rhythm. Not unconscious—a ball of pure consciousness. Arriving at the center, I weave without thought. I have no time to consider what color to add next. My hand is already on the shuttle.

When weaving, I prepare colors in almost wasteful abundance. The tone of a single color, the thickness of the yarn, strands tied together: forte, pianissimo, pizzicato. I need plenty of yarn before I begin, to ensure that I can capture the expression of color from moment to moment.

I can see the whole in my mind's eye, vaguely, but not the details. These come into view as I encounter them. With almost no straying, the colors form a melody. Those already woven crave the next. The next note longs to ring out. The moments that feel like crossing a gossamer mid-air bridge are when I hear the melodies of color most clearly.

Melodies of color

"Autumn excursion" (detail)

Complementary colors and optical mixing

Mother-of-Pearl

The painter Eugène Delacroix warned that green and purple should never be mixed on the palette. Blending complementary colors like these only results in a sleepy gray. Place green and purple side-by-side, though, and the magic of "optical mixture" creates a beautiful mother-of-pearl gleam—so I learned from the painter Oka Shikanosuke's book *An Offering of Flowers for France* (*Furansu e no kenka*). Just like a mosaic, if you paint different colors in close proximity and view them from afar, they seem to shimmer with life.

The same principle is at work in my weaving. For better or worse, the nature of weaving makes this inevitable. Strands of yarn cannot mix like paints on a palette. There is nothing for it but to take the purples and put them beside the greens.

I once received a compliment on the beautiful purple of a kimono I had made. When I explained that in weaving it I had only alternated red and blue threads—that there wasn't a bit of actual purple in it—I received only a mystified look in return, but such is the nature of complementary colors and optical mixing.

Work like this not only teaches us lessons that stay with us forever, it also becomes a bridge to our next challenge. The basic principles—the "habits"—of color, I learned not from painting but from weaving, where the fundamental law is that colors are not to be—indeed, cannot be—mixed.

Mother-of-pearl

Silkworms from Heaven

There is a sad and mysterious Japanese tale about silkworms. It is the tale of a girl and white horse who fall in love and ascend to heaven together, and one version can be found in *Legends of Tōno* (*Tōno monogatari*), Yanagita Kunio's 1910 classic of folklore studies.

The girl had known the beautiful white horse since her childhood. It was her only friend, and they ran through the fields and mountains together. The horse loved the girl too, never leaving her side. Eventually, as the girl grew up, she fell truly in love with the horse. The fact that it could not speak only made her feelings for it stronger and purer.

The girl's father grew suspicious of his daughter spending all her time in the stable. Eventually, he flew into a rage and killed the animal by hanging it from a tree. The girl embraced the horse's cold, white body and refused to let go. Still united, the two of them began to rise into heaven.

Watching his daughter fly away, the father yelled that he was sorry, and asked for her forgiveness. "Oh, no, Father," said the girl. "We aren't angry. Go into the garden tomorrow morning and look in the bowl of the mortar. What you will find there is our gift to you."

When the father checked the mortar the following morning, he found several white grubs squirming inside it. Each one had the head of a horse. He raised them with care, and when they finally wove cocoons around themselves, their silk brought wealth to the entire village.

In Japanese, the word for "silkworm" is written with the character 蚕, combining the glyphs for "heaven" (天) and "insect" (虫). What's more, for some reason, they are counted using the same word as large livestock—such as horses.*

---

* In Japanese as in other East Asian languages, numbers are expressed in combination with special words known as *counters*. The appropriate counter to use is determined by the thing being counted: there is a counter for people (*nin*), a counter for books (*satsu*), and so on. Most insects are counted using the counter *hiki*, but silkworms are counted using *tō*, which is normally reserved for larger animals like cattle and horses.

Gifts from the silkworm

Raw Silk

The traditional method of reeling silk from cocoons is called *zaguri* in Japanese, and the day I was taught to do it was the day I realized how pleasurable it can be. The basic work of making things always involves simple, repetitive actions, but they bring with them a deep joy.

The cocoons are white, beautifully rounded. They stand on tip-toe in the hot water together, spitting out their silk. The larvae inside have already entered eternal sleep, but now human hands tie dozens of strands together to reel them out as a single shining, translucent thread. As it comes, the thread still trembles with the motion of the silkworms, mindlessly bobbing from side to side. They have departed our world, using their own bodies to leave a gift for us: the thread of heaven. Raw silk, or *suzushi*.

Suzushi. It has a pleasing ring to it. The word evokes the domain of purity—of things untouched by any hand. That single shining thread contains the kind of cavities that only natural fibers do, which help preserve the warmth and moisture of human skin and allow the air to pass through. Before being twisted (*yori*) or degummed (*neri*), the newborn silk is almost stubbornly pure, and can be woven into sleek, translucent fabric.

The "Twilight Beauty" chapter of the *Tale of Genji* mentions "a charming young girl in long trousers of yellow *suzushi*," and this inspired me to make a yellow kimono of raw silk myself. I used gardenia, adding only a purple *ungen* design at the ends of the sleeves, and the result was as light and diaphanous as a cicada's wing. I worried that it was impractical, and held on to it for a while, but eventually it left me at the command of a certain beauty who wanted it for herself.

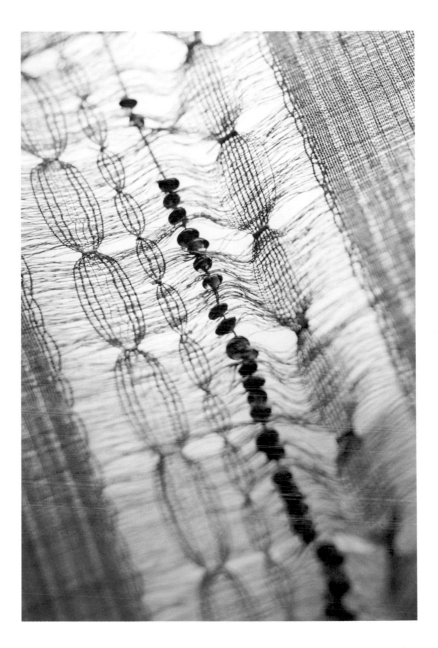

Suzushi *1*

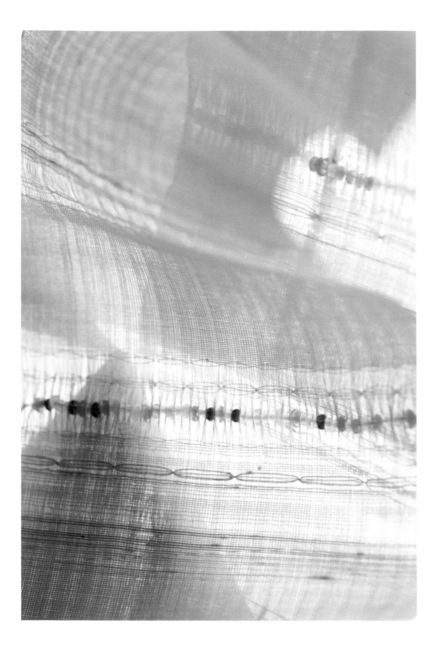

Suzushi 2

The Beauty of Plain Cloth

No pattern, no stripes or *kasuri*:* plain cloth is the most difficult textile to weave, because the fabric itself, the color itself, is all there is. Its original beauty. When ornamentation is swept away, true nature is revealed.

Thread selection, weaving technique—nothing can be left to chance. Still, when plain cloth truly captures the heart, it cannot be bettered.

Plain white cloth is the highest achievement of all. Not long ago, I saw evidence that spirits reside in such textiles with my own eyes. It was at Atsuta Shrine, where the sacred *togasane* (literally "ten-layered") *no onzo* garments have grayed with the dust of years but are thought to have been, long ago, whiter than white. The brilliant *togasane* fabric moved in a non-existent wind, and I felt a mystic sense of divinity.

The layered clothing favored by the nobility of the Heian period (794–1185) was endlessly elegant, too. "Siskin," "Cinnabar," "Wisteria," "*Hanada*," "Clove"—each refers to not just one color but a whole set of colors, worn in layers of plain fabrics to evoke the season. Here, too, the beauty of plainness is so superior that any pattern would be unnecessary.

I would like weaving some plain cloth to be my final work. I have spent many years absorbed in the pleasures of stripes, lattices, *kasuri*, *bokashi* washes, and *noshime* weaves, but I still long to weave a plain pongee of depth and richness, perhaps in indigo, or green, or scarlet. I dream of dyeing it a color that one can never tire of—a color beyond color entirely.

---

* *Kasuri* is the Japanese word for ikat, a technique of creating patterns in textiles by selectively dying the yarn and then aligning the colors while weaving.

Ivy leaves

Mordanting

Our finest colors show

On Mordants

Someone once described me as a weaver and dyer whose work had been fixed in me by the mordant of divorce.

Divorce is not often described this way, but what is mordanting if not change through suffering? Through mordanting, inborn colors are altered and entirely new colors are born. The same simmered plum branch dyes fabrics differently depending on whether the mordant used is lye or lime or iron.

Children grow up under their parents' influence, but eventually they come of age, marry, and find work, and their colors change with their environment. This process may not be as straightforward as dyeing fabric, but it, too, is a kind of mordanting. What colors do we take on when our essential nature encounters outside circumstances? Some people only shine more brightly when they suffer, while others are wounded and weakened. If only people, too, were able to choose the most suitable mordant to bring out their nature at its best.

To obtain the most natural and beautiful colors from a plant-based dye, lye made with charcoal from the same plant is best: plum lye for plum dye, sakura lye for sakura dye, and so on. Perhaps it is the same for people. Perhaps it is when we act as our own mordant and offer ourselves without reservation that our finest colors show.

Journey of light

Journey of Light

Nature reveals its secrets to anyone who pays close enough attention. In fact, they are not really secrets at all—only phenomena that we fail to notice because our minds are elsewhere. At these times, the sieve of our attention grows coarse, allowing even important things to slip through. But if some realization causes us to look more closely and think more carefully, the sieve suddenly grows finer. The countless grains that make up nature are unified under some system of order; an inner light reveals itself as it mingles and reacts with the light from outside.

I once held an exhibition in Ōita featuring almost a hundred pieces and visited the prefecture several times to prepare and rotate them. On my final visit, I chanced upon a patch of madder in the mountains and found myself digging up the roots so feverishly it was as if they were calling to me from underground. After that, I discovered madder each time I visited Ōita, from Kunisaki Peninsula to Shin'yabakei Gorge. What was it about those roots, which had slept in the earth for hundreds of years, that called out to me so? The dye they made was so pure that it shone—so unaffected that I hesitated and lost my way when it came time to weave it. Light in the soil, droplets shed by the sun into the earth, underground veins, or perhaps roots of light.

Goethe saw colors as the various expressions light took on as it entered the real world and met with circumstance. "Colors are acts of light," he wrote, "acts and sufferings." Reading these words for the first time, I felt as if an age-old mystery had been solved in an instant. Light is bent, divided, and made to reside in our world as color. We extract color from plants and dye it into fabric. Isn't this the same, at root, as the way we ourselves are colored by the phenomena we encounter and the suffering we endure in this world? Both could be called a journey of light.

Sometimes the light from the sun—source of all life—fills our world with all the beautiful colors to be found here. Sometimes it encounters unexpected obstacles, reaching us instead as shade and darkness. It dyes ores deep in the earth and penetrates to the roots of grasses.

I can only gaze in wonder at the colored light that lay within those madder roots I found in the mountains of Kyushu.

Madder roots

A Gray World

The Swiss artist Alberto Giacometti once said, "Gray is the basic tone of all colors. I like Paris because it is gray—just like life itself." In response, Japanese poet and critic Usami Eiji said, "Perhaps life is gray by nature, but if we think of our lives as three days, two gray and one rose-pink, the latter is surely the best day of our lives."

I wonder, though, if that rose-pink day might not also be seen through gray frosted glass.

Gray is, in fact, the basic tone of all plant-based dyes. When we simmer plant material, something always slips in with it—sap, perhaps, or some other impurity, casting a gray veil over the color we produce.

This is why plant-based dyes are often described as grounded or subdued. They contain impurities that cannot be crisply filtered out as they can be from chemical dyes, but this does not muddy their colors; on the contrary, their original nature is all the more striking.

Impurities in pure colors may sound like a contradiction, but it is the truth. Perhaps in this case we can say that the colors contain shadows. Gray is that shadowy part, that caring, kindly part.

Let me close with a poem I wrote long ago.

Into Their Garments

The gray I got from Seiryōji Temple's hisagi *
Was the color of the pigeons' wings
That flocked and flew about the temple gate and the pagoda

Pale gray, a hint of purple, a hint of brown
I let it spill from the drawer
A note half a tone flat, wreathed in thin evening mist
Accepting any color without complaint
A color that is kind beyond compare

Drawing the colors around it within
And showing them through itself
Placidly blurring
A gentle backlight

Would that I could
For women deep in suffering, in despair
Bodies broken, hearts broken
Wordlessly working
Weave into their garments just a hint
Of the kindness of hisagi *gray*

* Hisagi: *Mallotus japonicus*, or East Asian mallotus.

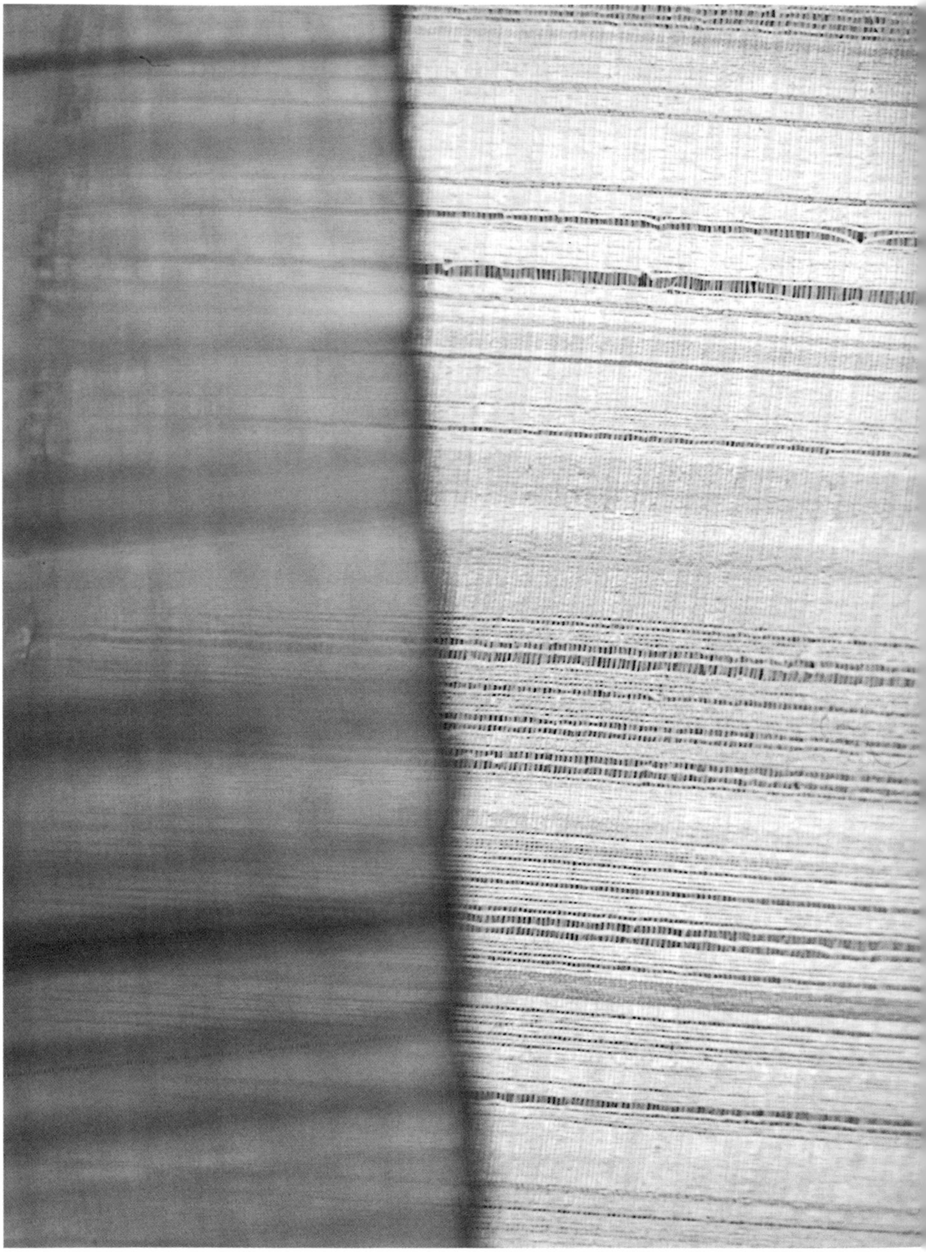

A gray world

Gleanings from the Sample Box

I have endless affection for fabric samples. The smaller they are, the more precious I find them. In my years as a weaver, I have created stripes of every kind—more than a thousand patterns, I am sure, although I have never counted. My collection of scraps and samples has long since filled my chest of drawers and spilled over into baskets and bundles wrapped in cloth. One day, I decided to pick out the patterns I was especially fond of and make a sample book.

As I gazed at the pieces of fabric spread out across the tatami mats, I began to hear voices whispering to me from here and there. Before long the room was filled with memories that rose from the samples like smoke from Aladdin's lamp.

I recognized scraps that had accompanied me on long journeys overseas. Scraps that had belonged to now-departed loved ones. Scraps like the last sighs of the Taishō period. Scraps like fragments of a mosaic. Scraps like a cross-section of marble. Scraps like streetlights in the rain. Scraps the color of red brick soaking up the autumn sun. Scraps like notes from a blue trombone. Scraps like fragments from an ukiyo-e print. Scraps like the wings of a bush warbler. Scraps like dappled snow on a paving stone. And so many more. The spindle of the seasons rolled slowly backwards and told its tale.

I chose fifty patterns and began to weave. Five years passed in the blink of an eye, rolls of fabric piling up one by one, and before I knew it I had a basketful. I was so careful when I took them out to gaze at them that people said I looked like I was handling some priceless, fragile treasure.

The next question was what sort of sample book to make. *Washi* paper pages with traditional Japanese binding? A Western-style volume with an embossed cover? A *kyōchitsu* wrapper made of bamboo strips, like the ones that are used to keep Buddhist sutras safe? In the end, I decided that the gentle sentimentality of the samples themselves would be shown to best effect by something quite the opposite—something metallic and hard. A silver-colored box with a glass window for a single scrap of cloth to float behind. I would display the box like a vase or sculpture, switching between my fifty chosen samples according to the season or the furnishings.

Finally it was time to cut the samples into shape. Taking scissors to them was not easy, but I snipped the countless pieces of fabric I had slowly collected over five years into little pieces. I wanted to recite the *nenbutsu* in apology. The samples to be put on display were fine, but the smaller leftover pieces and the long strips like cords I put in a cardboard box.

One day, I will use those scraps to make something beautiful. I will gather my beloved odds and ends together and make a small memorial pagoda to house these gleanings from the sample box.

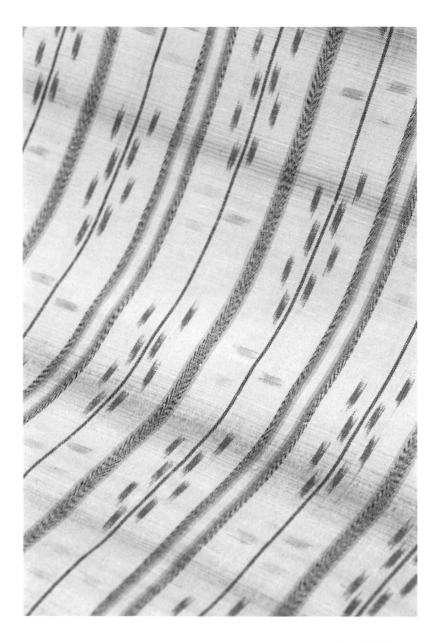

"Wind Bells" (Fūtaku)

Last Snows in Kohoku

Struck by an urge to see the snow on Lake Biwa, I boarded a train on the Kosei line, which runs northeast from Kyoto along the lake's western shore. The wind was cold, but it hinted at something beyond winter. When the lake came into sight, it was a dull gray color. A gentle spring seemed to be thawing.

But I had come to see the snow. I gazed across the water at the far shore, where Mount Mikami stood wreathed in mist. Had I just missed the end of the season? I was idly wishing I could summon it back when I happened to look away from the lake to the west. The Hira Range glimmered whitely in the far distance, while the powder-covered mountains just north of Kyoto itself looked like a copperplate print: a dark, densely etched vista in black and white.

I got off the train at Katata Station and made my way to Mangetsuji Temple, with its famous *ukimidō* or "floating hall" on the lake. It was surrounded by withered reeds, among which ripples on the lake's surface glinted as they caught the sun. Winter was long gone. I decided to return to the station and catch another train all the way to Nagahara at the lake's northern tip. The fishing weirs jutted out from the shore like the fletching of an arrow, making a *kasuri* pattern that has stayed with me for years now, though it has yet to take form in a weaving.

After we passed Imazu, the color of the lake changed. The sun's rays fell onto its surface through gaps in the clouds, and the dull gray began to give way to a crisp indigo.

There was a peculiar brightness to the solid white of the fields and the wild tangle of dry reeds along the shore. The yellow-brown haze of the reeds brought out the color of the lake beyond, which was like a vat of pure indigo, and the lake in turn transformed their yellowish brown into vivid gold leaf.

This was the work of the snow. Three spirits rose there, in indigo, gold, and white. When all that must wither has died, the surviving reeds sprout from the blanket of white, soft as an animal's fur.

With every station I passed, the snow grew heavier, deeper. I was headed into the heart of winter. Birds stood in white rice paddies that stretched to the shore of the lake. A wagtail took wing. Beside a murmuring stream, I saw the tracks of a field rabbit or perhaps a mouse striping the snow like the Okinawan twisted-yarn pattern called *mudi*.

Passing Makino Station and approaching the end of the line, the lake's color changed a third time, becoming a navy so rich and of such unsettling steely depth it was nearly black.

I saw the same eerie depth in the mountains, from this distance a scribbled mass of lines scratched out in black and white. They looked like gloomy monsters rooted to the earth. Human habitations clustered around those roots, huddled together and covered in snow. The train rounded the foothills and I saw fine sleet falling on the lake's northern shore.

The last station was unmanned.

Kohoku snowscape

"Last Snows in Kohoku" (Kohoku zansetsu*)*

"Moon in the Lake" (Tsuki no mizuumi)

"Signpost" (*Michishirube*)

When I first saw Frank Stella's metallic paintings, it felt like something was taking up residence in my soul. Perhaps I recognized some territory that I also laid claim to. I was unable to realize it in my work for many years, but the vision of that moment never faded—in fact, it only grew more solid.

I did not know what technique to use. *Kasuri* was the obvious answer, but I wanted to retain the metallic feel, and the slight misalignments of *kasuri* would have hindered that. It was impossible to create straight lines that suddenly turned at right angles through weaving alone. I would have to cut the threads.

Cut, and then retie. This would be an adventure, but once I saw that it was the only way, I did not hesitate. With intense concentration, I cut and retied the threads. It was simple work, but satisfying in a way that was quite new to me. Since I had not set foot in this territory before, I gave the piece I was working on the name "Signpost" (*Michishirube*). Success or failure, it would guide me toward the future.

Freed from my usual perspective bound by both Japanese tradition and the mechanism of the loom itself, I decided to take things as far as I could. When "Signpost" was complete, the final pattern was not quite the right size for a standard kimono, so I shortened the sleeves and raised the hem until the whole thing came only to ankle length.* The result felt something like the thick cotton kimonos known as *atsushi*, or even like a gown. It could be worn with *tattsuke-bakama* trousers, the kind that are snug around the ankle, or over slacks and a sweater with a leather belt. It inspired all kinds of unexpected ideas. I wondered, too, if the fact that it was about the right size to suit a tall Western man was another result of Stella's influence.

* Kimono for women are usually made somewhat longer than the wearer is tall, then adjusted to an appropriate length using folds at the waist.

First snow

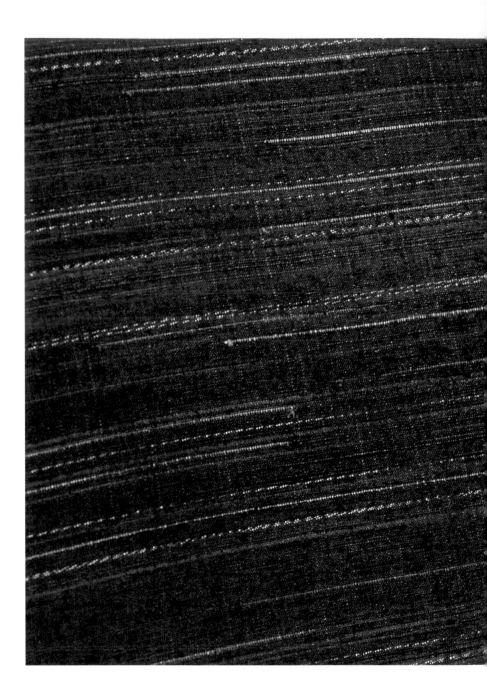

"Moon in the Lake" (Tsuki no mizuumi*) (detail)*

Snow—Deep North—Colors of the Requiem

My longstanding wish to visit the north was finally granted. When word came that the first snows there had started to fall, I was already prepared to set off.

In Kyoto it was still just warm enough to keep the autumn foliage at bay, so I thought the snow would be some time coming, but the night we arrived in Morioka in Iwate Prefecture I was informed that promising signs were already in the sky. This was from someone born in snow country, so it wasn't that I disbelieved them, but I was still taken by surprise the following morning when I sat at the front of a bus heading north on the Yodel route and saw flecks of white blowing against the windshield, as if the glass were drawing them in. It was the first snow of the year for me. I watched as a white veil was drawn across the mountains and fields that stretched out from both sides of the northbound expressway.

Disembarking the previous evening at Hanamaki, slightly south of Morioka, I had immediately felt immersed in the atmosphere of the writer Miyazawa Kenji's birthplace, as if my soul were being showered with invisible particles of his spirit. Sitting on that northbound bus, too, it was as if the glass had vanished and tiny homunculi were pouring from inside me, turning into white balls that dispersed into the air and mutely shouted *Kyrie, Kyrie,* or *Holy, Holy, Holy*. As I listened to this silent spiritual in the snow, I felt as if I were in prayer myself.

Why had coming to the north put me in mind of a requiem for the dead? Miyazawa's soul certainly dwelled in the memorial museum dedicated to him. The pure spiritual energy rising from the displays of his personal effects had moved me so deeply that it was difficult to leave, as if I had been pierced right through.

Before leaving Kyoto I had been reading a book by Makabe Jin called *Asura Beach: Gleanings from Miyazawa Kenji* (*Ashura no Nagisa: Miyazawa Kenji shū*). It was a collection of essays written over fifty-some years of studying Miyazawa and his work. Makabe lived in the same area as his subject, worked as a farmer himself, and had rare talent as a poet. I found the breadth and depth of his observations powerfully moving. The first snow I experienced in the north was also the first snow to fall on that foundation, which may explain why my breast filled with strains from Fauré's *Requiem*.

As the train through Hanamaki headed east toward Tōno, the mountains and fields along the Kitakami River were only scantly scattered with snow, but this was unmistakably Miyazawa's scenery, hazy with deciduous forests. About where the Kitakami and Sarugaishi rivers merge, I was gazing out the window thinking of the English coast when the train dramatically rounded the base of a mountain and new scenery came into view, making my heart beat faster.

Although I felt not a hint of the dismal in what I saw, I could not help recalling these lines from Miyazawa's short poetic cycle "Blue People Flow":

somo kore wa	And what is this,
izuku no kawa no	What river view
keshiki zo ya	Might this be,
hito to shibito to	That runs with people
murenagaretari	And the dead?

Such was the blue of the river water. It lacked the transparency of indigo; its base was sunken deep below. Along with the dappled white of the snowy banks and the golden brown of the dry grasses with their mysterious inner light, it formed a unity that made my chest tighten.

Why should these three colors dig into my soul? As I pondered the question, I heard a voice say, *The colors of the requiem*. Yes—that was it. My trip to see the snow on the northern end of Lake Biwa came back to me. There, too, the same three colors had left their mark on my heart. In the end, Lake Biwa is a presence in my life that I cannot separate from darkness and death. A lake of requiem.

From the northern shores of Lake Biwa, the water had been a steely, rich navy blue, so close to black it was almost eerie. Now Sarugaishi River was the color of Miyazawa's "Blue People Flow." Far ahead I saw beneath the stars an iron bridge with three arches, and I wondered if this might not be the real bridge of the Milky Way Railroad from Miyazawa's famous story.

It was a long way from Lake Biwa to Tōno, but having arrived I finally recognized my three primary colors. The rich navy, darkened until it approached the murky green of the depths; the golden brown of the dry grasses just about to bud into flower; and the pure fallen snow.

What else came to mind, there in the north of Japan? The memories of Arimoto Toshio, Kamoda Shōji, Onogi Gaku, Yamaguchi Kaoru, and Komai Tetsurō. All now departed, leaving such marvelous work behind. Their names were engraved on the golden leaves that fell slowly to the bottom of my breast. As the train pushed deeper north, the colors of the requiem grew all the more vivid.

The author with a sculpture by Arimoto Toshio

The Sakura of Fujiwara

Now that Ōoka Makoto's essay "The Power of Words" is in junior high school textbooks, I get letters from students every year.

One year, a teacher wrote to me from Fujiwara Junior High School in Gunma Prefecture. Her students had been fascinated by the essay's description of dyeing with sakura and wanted to try it for themselves—would I share the method?

Imagining this tiny school of just thirty-six pupils on the banks of Lake Fujiwara deep in the mountains, I immediately sent a reply, along with some yarn to dye. The students soon wrote back. They had gone into the woods and cut branches from the trees, but the dyeing simply had not worked out like mine did. Could they persuade me to visit them, just once? "We would all love to see you," the letter said. Like the first one, it was the picture of earnestness. It might have been the first letter of its kind the students had ever written. I could not help laughing at how lovely it was.

Yes, I decided—I *did* want to visit that school. By happy coincidence, the Gunma Museum of Modern Art was hosting a retrospective of my work that year, so I took the opportunity to visit Fujiwara as well. It was the beginning of March, when the snow was still deep, and I wondered if the car could even make it there. But, finally, past the lakes and valleys blanketed in white, I arrived at the school. The principal and even the mayor helped as we searched out and cut branches from trees in the snow: sakura, mizunara oak (*Quercus crispula*), dogwood, and kobushi magnolia. Once we had them all, we simmered them separately over burners in the science room.

Soon the room was filled with the rich fragrance of the branches. The smell was sharp and fresh, unmistakably redolent with the energy the trees had stored up in preparation for spring. Unable to wait for classes to finish, the students arrived. "Ugh, that stinks!" they said, red-cheeked with shyness, curiosity, and delight. Even the children who had toyed uncertainly with yarn skeins at first soon began to shine with life as they saw the strands take on the color of the dyes.

Finally, it was time to dye with the sakura. Sakura ash had already been prepared to make lye, and everyone held their breath as they watched my hands. The yarn that went into the sakura solution, mordanted by lye from the same tree, should have come out a faint but somehow still fragrant pink. What emerged instead was yellow tinged with red. A sense of disappointment spread among the students. "What's the *real* color of the sakura?" one of them asked.

"This is it," I told them. "This is the color of Fujiwara sakura." I could neither evade nor hide from the question. This, right here, was the very color of the branch we had found bent by snow yesterday and brought in. The sakura in the foothills of Mount Ogura in Kyoto might be pink, but those in the snows of Fujiwara were yellow. I confronted this fact before their very eyes, realizing my own presumption.

However, in their next letter one student described this in a wonderful way. "What stuck with me most vividly was that even dyeing with sakura does not give the same color every time, so there is no one color that you can say is the 'real' one. The sakura of Fujiwara are yellow: it makes me happy to think this. If you keep studying, you always find something true, which makes me even happier. I think that dyes are a kind of message from nature, and this is what the colors are trying to say to us. So I like dyeing very much now."

The students' young teacher wrote to me again as well. "Standing amid the harshness of nature, the trees bend all their efforts toward preparing to bud. Having received that vital energy along with their color and fragrance, we must listen to what they have to say to us, no matter what that may be. I see my students every day, but have I been paying enough attention to what they say? Have I heard the things they say without words? If we have not prepared a place for it on our side, the color loses its vitality. I feel that I have keenly understood this for the first time."

The response from the students was wonderful—just what I would expect from the undiluted sensitivity of those living in close contact with nature both gentle and severe. I will remember that glow of transparent wisdom, for the rest of my life. If I cast my mind back, I can still smell that sharp fragrance. It is the smell of those second-year junior high school students beginning to bloom.

On my visit to the school, I gave each of the students one bundle of yarn and asked them to dye it with the colors of Fujiwara's forests, fields, and grasses, and then send it back to me. Around the end of spring, the skeins began to return from the students. Horse chestnut, apple, peach, cherry birch, *sawagikyō* (*Lobelia sessilifolia*): they were like handfuls of spring itself.

I set up the yarn on my loom and began to weave. I did not need any design. The colors the children had found became stripes, and I used white yarn to add horizontal lines. When I was finished, I named this piece "The Snows of Fujiwara" (*Fujiwara no yuki*). Then I wove another, with the same warp but different weft: green for spring, indigo for summer, brown for autumn, and white for winter. From this I made a child's kimono, which I named "The Four Seasons of Fujiwara" (*Fujiwara no shiki*). When I visited Fujiwara Junior High School again to present it to them, the mountains blazed with deep crimson that shone off the lake below. The kimono is still at the school to this day.

Collecting the dye material

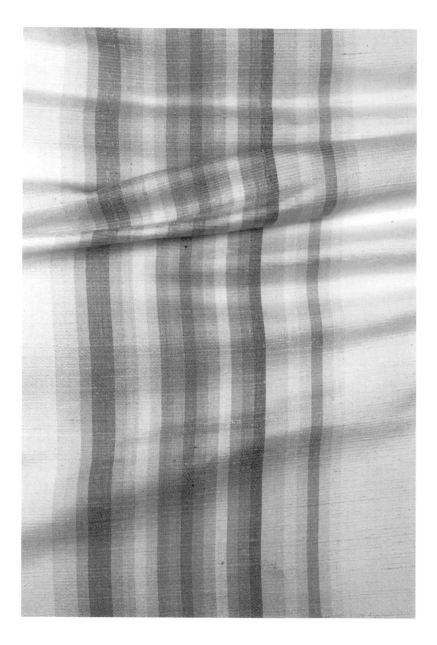

"Snows of Fujiwara" (Fujiwara no yuki)

Un, Kon, Don: Luck, Grit, and Simplicity

These words, like three jewels, were left to me by the late Kuroda Tatsuaki. I will never forget the sight of his broad white hands interlaced over his chest. All his life, they had sharpened blades, carved wood, and applied lacquer. As I gazed on them for the last time they seemed to me the very embodiment of his "luck, grit, and simplicity."

Kuroda always called himself maladroit, willful, and lazy, but I thought he had a rare intuition, frankness, and earnestness. This opposition, I think, is exactly where luck, grit, and simplicity emerge. Kuroda's public image may have been closer to his own assessment of his nature. All through the long years of obscurity and poverty before he gained public recognition, he never rethought his attitude to work, which does speak to a certain maladroitness in terms of life in general. No doubt those around him would have agreed that he was willful and lazy. But he carried on just the same, day by day.

One way of embodying simplicity is to repeat a process over and over despite having understood it the first time. Over the course of these repetitions, an essentially different understanding emerges. From within the wood emerges a Buddha, or perhaps a beautiful bowl. This unchanging persistence is connected to what we might call grit, and luck enfolds the whole. Luck is not happenstance: our accumulated daily effort summons it into being.

Luck, grit, and simplicity. When Kuroda first offered these words to me, I was in my early thirties. It was a difficult time in my life. I have now passed through my forties and fifties and am well into my sixties, and Kuroda's work inspired me to hold his words close to my chest the entire time.

A lacquered natsume *(tea container) by Kuroda Tatsuaki on fabric woven by the author's mother*

Top: Harlequin glory-bower fruit
Bottom: Alder cones

"Hisagi"

Tsumugi *and* Kasuri

Top: Yarn bundled and dyed for kasuri
Bottom: Warp yarn on the loom

Tsumugi and Kasuri

An editor from a certain publishing house was at my workshop the other day, looking at some of my work in *tsumugi* (a thin, soft kind of silk known in English as "pongee"). "What a pity," she commented, "that it can't be worn on formal occasions."

I have often heard this opinion voiced. *Tsumugi* is woven from yarn spun from silk floss, which is what remains in silk cocoons after the long, unbroken threads are extracted. It was what silk farmers kept to wear themselves. Small wonder that many dismiss it as inappropriate for dignified settings like the tea ceremony. But an old master who had pursued the "way of tea" further than most once confided to me that, if anything, *tsumugi* is the most appropriate type of kimono for that occasion.

How did *tsumugi* get its humble reputation? Its association with everyday wear is surely attributable in part to the unpretentious, warm feeling of the fabric itself. Translated to the language of ceramics, if formal *somemono* kimono* are porcelain, then *tsumugi* is earthenware. But, just as the potter Tomimoto Kenkichi invented a new kind of "half-porcelain" for the modern age that combined the smoothness of porcelain with the unpretentious heft of earthenware, I have long wondered if there could not be a "half-*tsumugi*" offering the warmth and comfort of *tsumugi* with the fineness of regular silk.

Before yarn production was standardized in factories, it was spun on simple machines known as *zaguriki*. You could feel the breath of the silkworms in that yarn. It had elasticity; it was alternately thick and thin along its length, rather than uniform. It was alive and beautiful, and it was perfect for "half-*tsumugi*." I have silk farmers in Nagano and Shiga spinning it for me already.

And, indeed, if you add just the right amount of yarn made from true silk floss to *zaguri* yarn, you can weave exactly the "half-*tsumugi*" I had in mind, neither inherently formal nor casual. Given the right design and color, these "half-*tsumugi*" kimono can be worn in any setting.

This, I believe, is how the kimono used to be. It was the wearer that mattered, not the perceptions of others. The mood of the kimono itself combined with the feelings of the person wearing it, moment by moment, day by day, creating a garment that could be worn with pride.

Kasuri, a fabric woven with yarn pre-dyed to create a pattern in the finished textile, is also considered inappropriate for formal occasions. The kind known as *kurume-gasuri* is the epitome of casual wear. It is made by binding yarn into tight little bunches, which are then dyed with indigo and aligned one by one on the loom. The work takes more patience than you might imagine.

Kasuri was not always such a humble fabric. *Dan-gasuri* and *noshime kasuri* were used in costumes for the Noh stage, outside of which *noshime* could only be worn by high-ranking samurai. In our modern age, however, *kasuri* is seen as so informal that outdoor workwear in navy *kasuri* (*kon-gasuri no noragi*) has become a stereotype.

I do not know of any other country that weaves *kasuri* designs as intricately intellectual as Japan's. And so, be it *tsumugi* or *kasuri* that I am weaving, I have resolved to ignore value systems imposed by others and continue combining the materials gifted us by nature with the best designs humanity can devise to create ever lovelier things to wear.

---

* *Somemono*, literally "dyed stuff," refers to kimono made from textiles dyed after they are woven.

Sappan red checks and a shuttle

"Lotus Lake" (Hasuike)

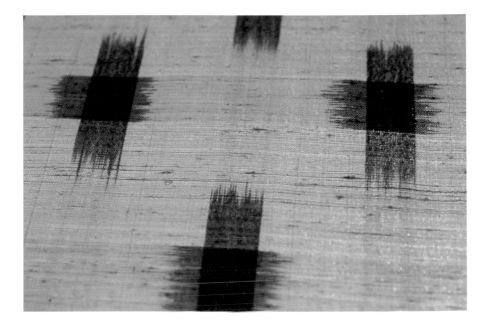

Kasuri *crosses*

Forty-Eight Browns and a Hundred Grays

During Japan's Edo Period (1603–1868), commoners were barred from wearing any colors other than brown, gray, or indigo. Their struggle to express individuality within these boundaries led to the creation of what were humorously referred to as "forty-eight browns and a hundred grays."

I first saw what this truly meant in a ragged old set of fabric sample books with an almost illegible title, which I eventually made out as *Fujiya Hanbei Dye Works*. Each volume had a hundred numbered fabric samples with names written in the fine Oie-style calligraphy used for official documents at the time.

There was "Summer-Clothes Brown," "Kite Brown" (after the bird), "Roof Tile Brown," "Rokō Brown" (after a famous kabuki actor), "Narikoma Brown" (another kabuki reference), "Goryeo Brown" (after the ancient Korean kingdom), and "Warbler Brown." The grays included "Fukagawa Gray," "Sekiya Gray," and "Saga Gray," named after well-known places, as well "Grape Gray," "Enshū and Rikyū" (two famous tea masters), "Pigeon's-Wing Gray," "Hooded Crane's Wing," "Pine Needle Gray," and countless more.

How am I to tell these "forty-eight browns and a hundred grays" apart? What sort of color does a name like "Enshū and Rikyū" conjure up? A sandy beach illuminated by the sun's last weak rays as it sets behind a pine, perhaps? I did sense something shadowy and complex in the hue. In musical terms, perhaps it was a microtone between *mi* and *fa*. Many of the colors had a certain irony to them— a touch of what is known in Japanese as *iki*, translated variously as "style," "chic," and "elegant detachment." The ability to distinguish the darker end of the spectrum to such an extent was surely cultivated in the Japanese by nature itself through the constant seasonal changes throughout the archipelago.

The philosopher Kuki Shūzō famously examined the use of brown and gray in his 1930 work *The Structure of Iki* (*Iki no kōzō*). *Iki* colors, he wrote, are "passive afterimages of dazzling experiences":

After tasting the full excitement of warmer colors, the soul seeks peace amid cooler tones as complementary afterimages. Iki *positions even colorblind gray within the bounds of the erotic; to be suffused with color, but unaffected by it, is* iki. *Within sensual affirmation,* iki *conceals a dark negation.*

The reason that brown and gray appeal to the Japanese as the most *iki* of colors, Kuki further argued, is because the structural characteristics of *iki*—eroticism, defiance, and detachment—are all concealed within them.

Thus did brown and gray become the colors of the witty, willful and worldly commoners of Edo, and indeed of all Japan.

Ungen-bokashi

My workshop looks out on Mount Ogura to the west, Mount Atago beside it, and, far off to the east, Mount Hiei. As the seasons change, their slopes are alternately blurred by haze that descends from above or wreathed in valley mist. Some days, when the sky is a clear and cloudless blue, they emerge so clearly that every leaf on their trees is distinct. Most of the time, however, they are shrouded in drizzling rain. From morning to night, I gaze out at their distant peaks every time my hands pause at the loom. The sunset behind Mount Atago is so magnificent I instinctively press my palms together in reverence.

I was gazing at these mountains surrounding Kyoto one day when I realized that the reason they bring me such endless joy is that each one is slightly different in hue. I was admiring not only their beautiful forms, but also their color palette.

Mountains upon mountains: from far to near, they gradually go from pale indigo-gray to rich indigo-green, just like the *ungen-bokashi* style of gradation used in Japan's decorative arts. The haze or mist— or sometimes rain or snow—that separates the layers only makes them more affecting. Beneath overcast skies, the mountains are as elegant as quietly waiting nobles with their garments trailing behind them.

You might call this the beauty of the *bokashi*, which on its own means simply "blurring," that arises when the humidity and precipitation of Kyoto combine with the slow wheel of the seasons. If the blessings of nature and the culture that received and fermented it have together created a unified realm of beauty, then *ungen-bokashi*, nourished by this country since the days of the Heian courtiers, belongs to this realm.

Indeed, the culture of the Japanese archipelago itself is a culture of moisture, like raindrops running down the leaves when humidity saturates the air.

Yellow Suzushi

Yarn dyed with murasaki *root*

Murasaki Shikibu and the Color Purple

Murasaki Shikibu is well known as the author of the *Tale of Genji*. I sometimes wonder if she used the roots of the plant whose name she shared—*murasaki*, or purple gromwell—to dye her own clothes. It does seem that the court women of her time did their own dyeing using plants both imported from overseas and gathered from nearby fields.

There is also a character called Murasaki in the tale itself, of course. She is adopted by Genji as a young girl, and he later comments on her skills as a dyer. The Lady of the Falling Flowers (known to Japanese readers as "Hanachirusato") is also praised for the colors she can produce.

In fact, you might say the color purple forms the core of the entire tale. Purple accompanies the narrative as it proceeds, intertwined with Genji's fate. His parents, the Emperor and Lady Kiritsubo, are both connected to the color in some way, as are Murasaki and her aunt, Lady Fujitsubo. Genji, the Shining Prince, is at the center of this group.

Yellow has always been the color of shining and light in Japan; it is also purple's complement. Like Genji and those around him, each shows the other to best advantage.

Purple gromwell root has been used for dyeing since ancient times. It is mentioned in the 8th-century *Man'yōshū*, the earliest anthology of Japanese poetry. The *Kokinshū*, another highly influential collection compiled in the early 10th century, contains the following poem:

Murasaki no	One purple
Hitomoto yue ni	Gromwell plant
Musashino no	Has made every blade of grass
Kusa wa minagara	On the Musashino plain
Aware to zo miru	Dear to me

Lines like these suggest an emotional parallel to the way that paper used to wrap fabric dyed with purple gromwell root will eventually take on a purple tinge as well.

In Murasaki Shikibu's day, people viewed purple as the noblest of colors, the ideal color. It often appeared in literary descriptions of clothing or possessions. Nevertheless, it seems to me a rare thing, even in world literature, for a single color to be intertwined so deeply with a story's characters and their fates—to be granted structural power as a framework for the entire tale—as purple is in the *Tale of Genji*.

Perhaps Murasaki Shikibu had a genius for seeing the mystical power of colors—purple in particular—and playing it against the souls of those sensitive to its power as she spins her tale.

Press the liquid out of *murasaki* root, use that liquid to dye with, and then mordant with camellia lye: a magnificent purple will result. However, if the dye is heated above 60° Celsius, that purple will hide itself away behind a dull gray cast. This gray is called *messhi* or *keshi-murasaki*: "disappeared purple."

The Murasaki of the *Tale of Genji* departs into *keshi-murasaki* in the chapter "The Seer." Genji follows suit in the following chapter, "Vanished into the Clouds," which famously contains no text except the title. *Keshi-murasaki* is a gray of mourning. That the fate of purple gromwell itself should connect with the tale's development and denouement in this way is just another example of Murasaki Shikibu's genius.

Keshi-murasaki *(disappeared purple)*

The Colors of Gion

One rainy day in the old capital, I happened on a line of ten or more *maiko** seeing someone off at Kyoto Station. With their velvet collars of pure black, navy *kasuri* raincoats, boldly exposed napes, trailing *darari* obi, shimmering hair ornaments, wooden *okobo* clogs with red straps, and various kinds of bamboo and oil-paper umbrellas, they were less beautiful than magnificent—an aesthetic crystallized and come to life.

Their diminutive forms were adorned to the point of saturation. They wore jeweled pins and flower combs in the gentle curves of their swept-up hair, goldwork in their "half-collars" (*han'eri*) of scarlet silk crepe, and *obidome* pins in their sumptuous obi that were laden with enough precious stones to put Art Deco jewelry to shame. Sleeves swaying like the robes of celestial maidens, they held up their kimono skirts as they hurried to their next engagement. They glanced back and doubled over with laughter together; whatever angle they were seen from, they were perfectly presented.

When a girl becomes a *maiko* at fourteen or fifteen, she wears her hair in the cheerfully decorated *ware-shinobu* style. At eighteen, she adopts the more subdued *fukumage*, and in the last month before graduating to full-fledged *geiko* she wears the elaborate but subtle *sakkō* coiffure. Is this not like petals scattering in the spring breeze? The flower of her youth is ornamented without mercy.

My kimono are worn by some of the greatest dancers in Gion, and I am always struck by the emotion they invest in their dress. They transfer to their kimono the feeling of living each moment on stage to the fullest. The way they wear each one, what they combine it with, and even the color of the hem lining is eye-opening. For a kimono with thin stripes on a white ground—a pattern known as "white rain"—these women can bring even a hem lining of indigo or wisteria or near-black eggplant beautifully to life.

The dancer Inoue Yachiyo** is said to have an exquisite eye for color when choosing kimono for the stage. She does not shy from tones that threaten to outshine her polished performances or extreme combinations that regular townsfolk could never pull off. Only those, like her, for whom art is life can get away with such daring decisions.

* A *maiko* is an apprentice *geiko*, which is in turn the word used in Kyoto for "geisha."

** *Inoue Yachiyo IV (1905–2004).*

Three-Span Aprons

Some summers ago, I was browsing the Tenjin market at Kitano Tenmangū Shrine when I came across a hemp kimono with a *kasuri* pattern in mesmerizing indigo. When I reached out to pick it up, I discovered that the other end was already in the firm grasp of one of Kyoto's famous female peddlers known as *oharame*. "I'm going to make aprons out of it," she insisted, refusing to let go. *Well, I want to wear it as a kimono*, I thought, but she added that it would make aprons for three, and I relinquished my claim.

The *oharame* apron is a distinctive one. The strings around the waist are decorated with colorful muslin, and the front is made of three separate panels, which explains the garment's name: *mihaba maedare*, or "three-span apron." They were originally worn by the ladies-in-waiting of the twelfth-century empress consort Taira no Tokuko when they went out to pick grasses and herbs in Ōhara, northeast of the city proper. The *oharame*—whose name literally means "women of Ōhara"—admired these outfits so much that they made their own to wear when they went into Kyoto to sell kindling.

I have made a number of these aprons myself. They have an elegant yet brisk air about them and skillfully conceal minor dishevelment of the kimono as its wearer moves, making them ideal for work at the loom. *Kasuri*, stencil printing, dyed colors: I have quite a collection of designs, all a joy to mix and match with kimono for everyday wear, receiving special guests, or just to mark the passing seasons.

Kimono and Obi

Recently, I saw a store advertising a full kimono set for sale. The display included everything from *nagajuban* (inner robe) and *han'eri* collar to obi (sash) and *obijime* (cord for keeping the obi in place). The color and design had a subtle, overripe languor in the Taishō Romantic mode of the 1910s and 1920s. For a moment, I thought I was looking at clothing for some oversized doll. But I suppose this is what young people find appealing these days.

They no longer know the pleasures of finding the right kimono accessories one by one and using them to create new ensembles. Today, everything must be sold pre-coordinated, so the buyer can tell herself, "Yes, I could pull that off." This might be for the best, since people now wear kimono once a year or so at most. Speaking as someone who wears them all year round, however, this is not what kimono truly are.

A kimono–obi combination is like an inseparable married couple, or perhaps simply the bond between any man and woman comfortable in each other's company. The beloved obi that wraps up a favorite kimono, the *obiage* that helps keep the bow in place and the *obijime* that adorns the front: this is the wonder of conversation. The kimono draws the obi near while feigning indifference, and the obi holds tight with an expression it reveals only to the kimono.

Obi are capable of metamorphoses that surprise even me. I have favorites that I have worn for decades, and they still show me new faces. The same is true of kimono: investing the right emotion in the color of a *han'eri* can infuse any occasion with a hint of sensuality.

I once made an obi from old fabric specifically to go with a pomegranate *obidome* by Tomimoto Kenkichi that I inherited from my mother. While sewing the obi, I gave no thought to the person I might wear it for. It was for the *obidome* alone.

Reserved sentiment, or something very close to it, is at the heart of every kimono. The most important supporting role is played by the *nagajuban*, which reveals itself in glimpses at the wrists and *furi* (the openings under the sleeve). To be wrapped in this secret allure is something I find most enjoyable.

Many years ago, I spent much of my time with the painter Kobayashi Kokei's daughter Tsū. "O-Tsū-san," as I called her, was brusque by nature, not at all inclined to false praise, and her eyes were so clear they were almost blue. Her kimono preferences were absolutely her own, and she knew herself very well.

For kimono she liked designs that were free of ostentation, fusing *iki* (chic) with class, but her *nagajuban* were always evocative. Gray stripes on dark red; indigo dotted with brown and white flowers in chintz-like patterns—the beauty seemed to spill from her cuffs. Her obi, which she tied with artful carelessness, were sewn from vintage textiles of mysterious origin, not to be found for sale anywhere; I suppose her father bought them overseas. Her outfits were the product of her own eye. She wore them with pride, and her passion burst irrepressibly through.

I still think back fondly on our friendship. It has been almost a decade since she passed on.

Top: "Waiting for the Moon" (Tsukimachi) (left) and "Kume Island Kasuri*" (Kumejima Kasuri) (right)*
Bottom: Yarn stock

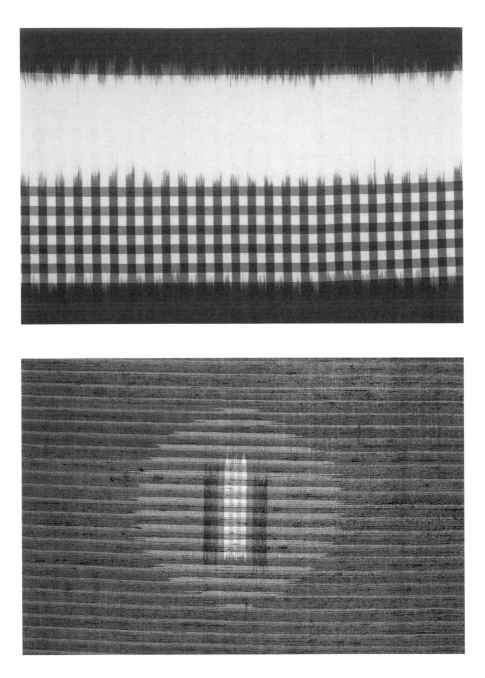

Top: "Purple and White Levels" (Shihakudan)

Bottom: "Snowlight" (Yukiakari). Yarn dyed with Bungo plum

The Art of Accessorizing

Combs, pins, and other adornments for the hair. *Han'eri* half-collars. *Obiage, obijime,* and *obidome. Tabi* socks and *zōri* sandals. Except for the artists who create these accessories, only the women who wear them know the passions invested within. The smaller the piece, the more intensely this sentiment is concentrated, until it almost becomes a part of the wearer's soul.

In some accounts, Cleopatra is said to have ended her life using a hairpin that had poison concealed within. Okinawan women, too, wore hairpins that could be used to take their own lives—or to defend them, as a weapon of last resort.

Hair and its adornments can be powerfully symbolic of women themselves. In the early Shōwa period in particular, the 1920s and 1930s, hair ornaments embodied the mode of the times. Velvet, ivory, tortoiseshell, precious metals, coral—all were put to use in creations that went beyond traditional natural motifs like flowers and birds to embark on wild flights of fancy. The designs often evoked exotic lands, with images of globes, gas lamps, and foreigners themselves, but there were also more familiar motifs: turnips and broad beans, kettles, mice, and even cheerful "*Yajirobē*" balancing toys. All remain marvelous treasures to this day, but I doubt any would have occurred to makers of hair ornaments in the West.

The Taishō period (1912–1926) was the golden age of the *han'eri.* Chests-of-drawers were made just to hold half-collar collections, and sending one to a woman was the first step in wooing her. I can still vividly recall one example I saw which featured an exquisitely drawn black snake frolicking in a spring field. The skillful execution suggested a male artisan of the underworld—but I wonder whose breast it adorned?

Obiage and *obijime* hold the obi in place at its vital points. I can well remember seeing a friend of mine in a black obi with a purple fawn-spot (*sō kanoko*) *obijime* and an ivory *obidome* in the shape of a traditional Noh playbook.

White calico *tabi* so snug on the feet that the seam leaves a clear impression on the instep when they are removed; the whisper of their approach down a corridor: there is something unique to Japanese womanhood in this.

A row of three pairs of *zōri* in a *genkan* entranceway freshly purified with water for guests. The first pair was mustard colored, with *hanao* straps of red, purple, and gray. The second was red lacquer with *hanao* of siskin green trimmed in crimson. The third had a sole made of straw and tie-dyed purple straps. Together, they evoked the world of early 20th-century *Nihonga* paintings in miniature, or perhaps, to a visitor from overseas, an abstract painting. Theirs was the beauty of equilibrium between color and shape—of artisanship that adorns the foot with quiet dignity.

The Future of the Kimono

Why has Japan abandoned the kimono? Among the traditional necessities of life—clothing, food, and shelter—the kimono was the first to be relinquished, and not with any sign of regret, either. Japanese food, on the other hand, is increasingly popular abroad. I was surprised to learn that Paris has nearly fifty Japanese restaurants.

The kimono's ongoing demise has many causes, and I do not believe anything can be done about them. Rather than see "new kimono" or clumsily simplified or Westernized versions, I would rather the kimono remain as it is, however far its stock may fall.

On the other hand, I have no objection to the kimonos I make being worn belted over sweaters and the like. This is an inconsistency, but necessary in its way. The direction of the times is clear, however lamentable we may find it. If I can help maintain high standards for kimono themselves, that is enough.

The idea that kimono are not compatible with our era implies, conversely, that they conceal within them the essence of great beauty. Their sleeves, their obi, and their waist folds (*ohashori*) all call to mind the "usefulness of the useless" expounded in the *Zhuangzi*. Here is where the allure of the kimono lingers.

The importance of the sleeves to romantic encounters in ages past can be seen in phrases that remain in use to this day. To offer just a handful, there is *sode no tsuyu*, "dew of the sleeve" (that is, tears); *sode no shigarami*, "weir of the sleeve" (against the flow of tears); *sode no ka*, "fragrance of the sleeve" (intentionally imbued with incense, to make an impression); *sodeshigure*, "autumn shower on the sleeve" (again, of tears); and *sode no wakare*, "parting of sleeves" (after a night spent on both partners' kimonos, spread out side-by-side with sleeves overlapping).

Ohashori is perhaps a less familiar word to the youth of today, but a kimono's waist folds are where the wearer reflects their mood for the day. When preparing to buckle down and work, a relatively high hem and snug upper body fit are better, while a longer hem and looser fit can lend a more convivial impression when meeting with a special someone. How we wear our kimono seems to change of its own accord depending on the occasion.

Though all the same shape, kimono have a thousand faces depending on the mood and circumstances of the person within. The height of the obi alone—up under the breasts or down around the waist—reveals the wearer's environment and even occupation. Seemingly unnecessary details in fact serve as a way of deeply enfolding a woman's emotions while still rendering them visible from without.

Many young people today—a surprising number, in my view—think of kimono as both formidable opponents and living things, best avoided rather than embraced. But, conversely, as long as this instinctual respect for them flows in the blood of the Japanese, kimono will never die.

What will kimono be like fifty or a hundred years hence? Pondering this question, I feel like a mother praying from afar for her beloved child's future.

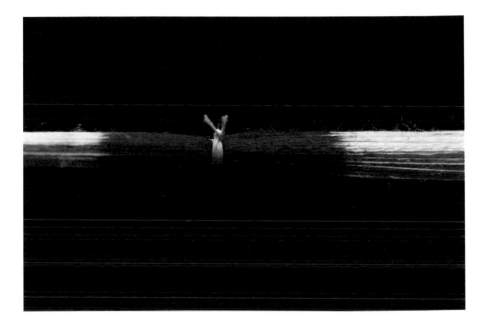

Sappan red kasuri *yarn*

Half a Life in Sappanwood Red

The New Year after I turned sixteen was a fateful occasion for me: the day I finally learned about my birth. My biological father, who had arrived in Tokyo at the end of the year, brought me back to my first home in Ōmi, where he and my birth mother revealed everything at the bedside of my gravely ill brother. The winter light came in under the deep eaves, down the corridor, and through the paper *shōji* screen to sink into walls the color of dried grass. The room was dim, and the New Year's decorations were plain and dignified.

I remember playing a game called "Camouflage" with my birth mother and other family members during that period. It involved each person obscuring their identity and writing a short response to a prompt, which the others would use to try to guess who had written it.

The prompt "Red" came up. Perhaps because I was young and it was the first time we had all been together like that, I was in an extremely lofty mood. The word "Red" evoked in me an image of absolute intensity, so I wrote *In this world, there is no true red*. I had just learned my birth mother's true identity, a meeting too fateful to fill the sixteen-year blank at once, and "Red" seemed to have appeared before me as some kind of symbol. Later, my mother told me that when she read my words she, too, felt she had been dealt a card of deep import.

I never dreamed then that a dozen or so years later I would be dyeing things red myself.

Even among red dyes, sappan is an outlier. It does not grow in our country and must be imported from far-off India or Malaysia; as it simmers, it fills the room with mysterious fragrances and heat from the tropics, intoxicating me with the spirit of redness. I fell under sappanwood's spell and simmered and dyed for days as a small pile of used-up wood accumulated behind my workshop. After I hung the crimson-dyed bundles of thread out to dry in the garden, I would go out to look at them over and over again—often running into my mother, there for the same reason. "You're back again?" we would say to each other, laughing together.

In retrospect, my mother must have been even more enchanted by sappan than I was. Dissatisfied with the reds I had obtained, she used vast quantities while I was away in Tokyo to produce what must have been the deepest possible crimson.

I used that yarn to weave an obi. To this day, my heart churns uneasily with a deeply emotional red when I hold it. Perhaps you could call it the color at a woman's core.

Deep red, rich crimson, maroon, false purple—sappan shows many faces, depending on the mordant. It is the changing form of woman herself, from harlot to saint. Not for nothing do I call sappan red the irresistible color.

I once dyed a length of fabric a red that was simply too raw   too much like my own past self, with a certain purity but haughty and arrogant, ignorant of true suffering. I could not bear it, so I decided to stain the fabric. I dyed it again with bayberry brown, and this gave the red a firm grounding. It became the color of a woman who had tasted bitterness. It embraced other tones with a warmth it had never shown before, like a woman who had bowed low to enter at the gate of another household as a new bride and wept helplessly, heedless of who was watching, at the lessons of human sentiment.

This was when I was just past the age of thirty, recently divorced, and realizing that with no one else to turn to I would have to provide for myself. My place as a housewife, pliant and unexceptional, had evaporated; left with no choice but immersion in my inner life as a woman, I confronted sappan red, losing myself in it as proof of life. I was possessed by its ever-changing ways and bent to its will. Sometimes the struggle was so fierce that I passed out from exhaustion.

But that was merely my physical form, and my eventual recognition that the reds of this world, including my distrust of other women— or perhaps of myself—were ceaselessly in flux left the thought *In this world, there is no true red* engraved deeply on my soul.

At sixteen, the curtains rose on my life. In that new dawn, I saw an unearthly omen in bright crimson. I put my sense that it was not of this world into those words, and those words have stayed with me, unchanged, for more than forty years. I have reached the age where the passion around red fades and one can only watch the flowers fall—so why, I wonder, do I sense the presence somewhere of that bright crimson omen again?

Sappan red kasuri *yarn*

Afterword to the Paperback Edition: The Work Does the Work

At the beginning of my thirties, I lost the entire foundation of my life. I left my two young children in the care of my adoptive parents in Tokyo and returned to the home of my birth in Ōmihachiman, where I began learning to weave. I had learned to use a loom in my teens, but really I knew nothing of weaving, yarn, or dyes—I was just a housewife like any other, forced out into the world to fend for myself. Looking back, the situation I was in appears quite wretched, but somehow it felt fresh to me at the time. This was work I could do as a woman on her own, making my time my own from morning to evening. I was truly fortunate that my birth parents, with whom I lived, were in good health. Each day, carrying a packed lunch my mother had made, I walked down a path where yellow roses bloomed to a humble weaving workshop outside the village. The married couple who owned it were poor, but kind, and they taught me my trade. My first creation was *sakiori* or "rag weave": an old scrap of red silk in a warp of vermillion yarn. When I finished, I raced back up the path to show my mother. In retrospect, that *sakiori* was beautiful. The silk was a pale crimson, and the green was dark yellow, and the cinnabar red that was scattered across it gave it the look of an abstract painting. That was the first thing I wove, and where all my work began.

Forty years later, I have done more weaving than I can recall. I was always surrounded by young people—three or four, sometimes seven or eight—and together we tirelessly wove kimono after kimono. When I woke up in the morning, the work filled my breast until it seemed it might burst. Before I knew it, I was at my workshop, finishing the design, dyeing the yarn in the dyeing shed, winding the yarn, setting the warp, and then sitting down at the loom to weave in the weft. This went on day after day, and now I am past seventy, realizing with a start that all that work was done *by the work itself*. At half past eight, the clack of the loom has already begun. Steam rises from the tubs in the dyeing shed. Yarn goes into the dye with a "One, two, three!" The spindles turn, the *kasuri* is bundled, and the pattern decided; the work calls, leaving us no time even to pause for breath. People working with pleasure in the shadow of the work; surroundings and repetition: these are the elements that have made things, and that have formed the story of this past forty years. How would it have gone had I been working alone? I doubt I would have spun like a spindle from eight in the morning to six in the evening. My young co-workers never miss a day and busily set about their tasks.

"What should we do here? Dye some more yarn? I must go and gather some of those grasses . . ." The next warp, the next design, the next job is always waiting. When the fabric is finally done, my co-workers cradle it reverently as they run it through hot water. Their faces as they wrap the dyed cloth in a towel are like those of young mothers swaddling an infant after its first bath. They set the loom's tempo and use one another as dressmaker's dummies. Once the kimono is ready, they place it on a hanger and nervously call me in.

"Oh, that came out nicely." When these words come from my heart spontaneously, relief and happiness fill their faces. The finished product is work we have done together. Without deep mutual understanding, it would be impossible. Even as I strive to bring out their best, I rely on their support. The work does the work, but in the gaps there are people, hands joined, always doing their best, never letting their concentration or motions falter. And if my young co-workers should err, this, too, is fine; I think only of how to make it right and move on. Put another way, there are no mistakes: whatever path we took was the only one we could have taken. It was the road to where we are. This also applies to my own life. What must have seemed a great mistake, a setback, and a failure to other people was the beginning of my work. Without that setback, I might still be a housewife like any other. Instead, I spend my days thinking not about the people in my neighborhood but about the materials in my workshop and building deep, deep relationships with them. My hands, the sensation in my fingers, speaks to the yarn. It is the material that chooses me. In the past, it often pushed me away or turned its face from mine and refused to speak. But after a point, it began to cling to me. The many expressions of the material emerge from the depths of the weave: sometimes a reserved smile, sometimes a harsh scolding that cuts sorely. I must never slacken my efforts to help the material rest easy there.

The same is true of colors. Even more than materials, colors are an intangible, uncertain presence. They are not things. For me, they begin to exist as colors and to have a sense of presence above other things only when they penetrate the yarn and become one with it. They are not pre-existing; I am always creating them.

I have been compared to a paint manufacturer. Others have asked why I insist on making my own colors when color can be bought at a store. But the colors I use are not available for sale, any more than I am. They are like children: they choose me, come to where I am. In a sense, they are entrusted to me, and although I do create them, their deepest roots are something I receive.

I have used this phrase, "receiving color," for many years. When I see it now, my reaction is *Enough. The time for those words is over.* When I hear it, I think *Not again!* It is not that I recant the idea, but I feel frustrated at how long I have let those words hold me back. I want to tell myself to stop all this "receiving" and think. What lies beyond where I am?

Whatever it is, I have set out for this great beyond already. Perhaps I have already arrived. For forty years and more, I never worked alone, not for a single day. My young co-workers and I did everything together, sharing conversations and explorations, discoveries and joy. We enjoyed each other's company. We were a community, even when we numbered just four or five. This was where the work was born, and if "the work did the work," our community was what made it happen. It was not me as an individual. That, I realized at last, is the true essence of craft: it arises from many people's wisdom, many souls, never just one. Colors were received, materials were received, but it was the vessel of the community that allowed them to thrive.

I have finally begun to understand what Yanagi Sōetsu meant when he spoke, as he often did, about guilds, saying, "We must unite our aspirations, raise the banner of our ideals, and build the kingdom of crafts." It seems to me that this was a common refrain of his, but I never felt as if my work had involved aspirations or ideals—just a handful of people entertaining themselves. But to keep that up for so long and still not tire of it—to want to keep pushing on together—if this is not an aspiration, then what is it?

I have finally begun to understand Yanagi's true ideals: to immerse oneself for an entire lifetime in something, some calling, and to base one's life and work on clear ideas. How else could they be sustained? When I began my own work, I read Yanagi's *The Way of Crafts* (*Kōgei no michi*) and found my way of life there, and those ideals have lived within me ever since.

Each day I seek to draw one step closer to those ideas rather than straying from the path. I could speak of what I like, what I enjoy, but this would be too shallow; these ideas contain a bottomless truth whose light has always given me comfort and strength. How else could the work do the work? The work and I were like the two wheels of a cart. Or, no—we were like a single wheel together, conjoined and inseparable.

The philosopher Rudolf Steiner said, "Every idea which does not become your ideal slays a force in your soul; every idea which becomes your ideal creates within you life-forces." So, are my own ideas becoming ideals? To be honest, I do not know myself. I certainly hope so, but I must not look at what I do through rose-colored glasses. The merest slip of the hand on the tiller can send the boat in entirely the wrong direction.

In today's world, there are no ideals. There are only fantasies. When I arrive at the brink like this, unable to quite step off, I remember

Steiner's words. The part of my work that is overdone affectation rises, and my motivation begins to sink. Ideas and ideals vanish from before me, and I soon feel like a water wheel, still spinning with inertia. There is no such thing as an ideal without an idea. Any article of faith worthy of being called an idea that I can truly hold must be an ideal too. Accordingly, there is also no such thing as an idea with no ideal. I believe they are one. Have I really managed to hold ideas about this work? That is the largest question remaining for me.

"The work does the work": I wrote this without thinking, but when I returned to Yanagi's comment in "The Dharma and Beauty" (*Hō to bi*) on the *nenbutsu*, or traditional chanting to Amida Buddha as an expression of faith in Pure Land Buddhism— "The *nenbutsu* chants the *nenbutsu*"—I realized how conceited I was being, and my entire body blazed with embarrassment. I wanted to rewrite the entire essay. Originally, these were reportedly the words of Ippen Shōnin, the thirteenth-century Buddhist preacher. How appropriate that one whose behavior was as pure as Ippen's was first to arrive at these truths: "the *nenbutsu* chants the *nenbutsu*" and "the Name hears the Name." The words are unsuitable for the mouth of an impure human like myself.

Yanagi offers the example of "landscape teapots" (*sansui dobin*) from Mashiko. They are the most everyday of folk crafts, but the painters work so quickly and unceasingly that they create thousands of landscapes, tens of thousands, without even remembering what they paint or how. When they enter that state, the painting itself does the painting: the work does the work, and human and work are at some point united.

Discovering this, I realized just how rose-colored my glasses are when I examine my own work. I will not deny that this came as a shock.

But having weathered that shock, I feel as if my eyes have begun to open.

In Sympathy with Nature (Inoue Takao)

In the mountains or in the fields, an encounter with a single leaf can evoke boundless nature in its entirety.

The space of modern culture, with its dizzyingly rapid development, has given birth to a bizarre rationality, a slanted set of assumptions, and a self-centered aesthetics: human greed gone much too far. And yet it seems to me that nature's original visage still calls to us, urging us to think again.

For the past several years, I have spent even more of my time than usual in the wild, far from human habitation. Is there something within me that makes me do this?

When I view the ever-changing natural world through my camera's viewfinder, I always feel admiration for those who dye with the grasses and trees. I imagine the profundity of a world of connection to nature in which one does not dye with its colors but rather is dyed by them. In photographic terms, it is the difference between shooting nature and simply allowing the retina or film to be suffused by colors and forms arriving on boats of light.

To me, releasing the shutter in nature feels like being roused and returned to the viewpoint of a human who has been saved—to the womb of nature, if you prefer.

We humans have a long history within nature, but we remain ourselves nonetheless. Sympathetic exchange with nature is an essential nutrient for us.

Colors and shapes that feel born from awe of nature or mysterious encounters with it; forms that evoke natural visages or presences sensed rather than seen: the beauty and vitality that flow from trees to make dyes and fabrics might be found in these things. Perhaps the rhythm of nature and humanity at work is where we must look to discover our future.

The creations and aesthetics of Shimura Fukumi constitute a marvelous but entirely human voyage.

In sympathy with nature

Shimura Fukumi

Born in Ōmihachiman, Shiga, in 1924, Shimura Fukumi received her first lessons in weaving from her mother at the age of 17. She began working with plant-based dyes in 1955. Recognized as a Living National Treasure by the Japanese government, she has also received the Osaragi Jirō Prize and other literary awards for her writing on art.

Inoue Takao (1940–2016)

Photographer Inoue Takao was born in Shiga in 1940 and graduated from Kyoto City University of Arts in 1965. Folk crafts, Buddhist art, the city of Kyoto, and the natural world were among his favorite subjects. His published collections include *Tibetan Esoteric Murals* (*Chibetto mikkyō hekiga*), *The Modern Tea Ceremony* (*Gendai no chakai*), and more.

Matt Treyvaud

Translator Matt Treyvaud was born in Australia and lives south of Tokyo. Recently published translations include Takashina Shūji's *The Japanese Sense of Beauty* and Minagawa Hiroko's *The Resurrection Fireplace*.

〈英文版〉色を奏でる
The Music of Color

2019年3月27日　第1刷発行

著者　　志村ふくみ
写真　　井上隆雄
訳者　　マット・トライヴォー
発行所　一般財団法人出版文化産業振興財団
　　　　〒101-0051 東京都千代田区神田神保町3-12-3
　　　　電話　03 5211-7282（代）
　　　　ホームページ　http://www.jpic.or.jp/
印刷・製本所　光村印刷株式会社

定価はカバーに表示してあります。
本書の無断複写（コピー）、転載は著作権法の例外を除き、禁じられています。

Copyright © 1998 by Fukumi Shimura and Takao Inoue
Printed in Japan
ISBN 978-4-86658-061-6